ZEN NAVIGATION FOR POST-PANDEMIC OFFICE DYNAMICS

FIGHT, FLIGHT, OR FELLOWSHIP

SAMUEL C MARTINEZ

This book is dedicated to Ruth J. Martinez and each employee that plays a role in building the world we share, often unseen but always felt.

Every page of this book carries the essence of dedication—

much like the unwavering commitment of every worker, from freelancers charting their course to those in multinational corporations.

May your contributions consistently be recognized and celebrated.

CONTENTS

Foreword	vii
Introduction	ix
Chapter 1	1
Chapter 2	7
Chapter 3	23
Chapter 4	35
Chapter 5	43
Chapter 6	47
Chapter 7	53
Chapter 8	57
Afterword	63
Thank you	65

Zen Navigation for Post-Pandemic Office Dynamics, *Fight, Flight, or Fellowship*

Published by Samuel C Martinez

Copyright © 2023 by Samuel C Martinez - All rights reserved

Logo by Greg Del Hierro

The content within this book may not be reproduced, duplicated, or transmitted without direct written permission from the author or the publisher. Under no circumstances will any blame or legal responsibility be held against the publisher, or author, for any damages, reparation, or monetary loss due to the information within this book, either directly or indirectly. You are responsible for your own choices, actions, and results.

Legal Notice:

This book is copyright protected. This book is only for personal use. You cannot amend, distribute, sell, use, quote, or paraphrase any part, or the content within this book, without the author's or publisher's consent.

Disclaimer Notice:

Please note the information within this document is for educational and entertainment purposes only. All effort has been executed to present accurate, up-to-date, reliable, and complete information. However, no warranties of any kind are declared or implied. Readers acknowledge that the author is not rendering legal, financial, medical, or professional advice. The content within this book has been derived from various sources. Please consult a licensed professional before attempting any techniques outlined in this book.

By reading this document, the reader agrees that under no circumstances is the author responsible for any direct or indirect losses incurred because of the information within this document, including, but not limited to - errors, omissions, or inaccuracies.

ISBN: 9798861136105

FOREWORD

Zen is a profound philosophy and spiritual practice that invites individuals to cultivate mindfulness, inner peace, and self-awareness. It emphasizes being present in the moment, transcending the limitations of the ego, and experiencing a deep sense of connection with oneself, others, and the universe. In Zen, one seeks enlightenment through meditation, self-reflection, and realizing one's true nature.

Embracing a Zen life means living with intention, simplicity, and mindfulness. It involves letting go of attachments, quieting the mind's constant chatter, and finding contentment in the present moment. A deep sense of inner calm, compassion, and a harmonious connection to the world characterizes a Zen life. It encourages self-discovery, personal growth, and pursuing a balanced and fulfilling existence.

The registered ZEN4 logo is a visual representation of the journey of personal development within the context of Zen philosophy. Each letter in puzzle format conveys the stages of growth and transformation that individuals undergo as they delve into Zen study and integrate its principles into their daily lives.

The "Z" is divided into four pieces, representing the initial stages of exploration and self-awareness. As one progresses, the "E" comes into focus with its three pieces, symbolizing the deeper insights gained through contemplation and mindfulness. The "N" follows with two pieces, signifying the refinement of one's understanding and cultivating a harmonious existence.

The number "4," solid and darker in color, is a testament to accomplishment and personal growth. It highlights the stages of development and the milestones reached through diligent practice and introspection. However, the solidity of the "4" does not signify a final destination. Instead, it reflects the continuous journey toward greater awareness and enlightenment.

The ZEN4 logo on the cover of this book beautifully captures the essence of Zen philosophy—a path of evolution, self-discovery, and inner transformation. It serves as a reminder that while each stage brings its rewards, pursuing enlightenment is a lifelong journey characterized by ever-deepening levels of wisdom, bliss, and self-realization.

INTRODUCTION

The health of your workforce is the heartbeat of your company, and the rhythm of their relationships sets the tone for your success. - Unknown.

The Covid-19 pandemic stormed into our lives much like the lyrics of Miley Cyrus, "I came in like a wrecking ball." Covid-19 shocked the direction of our lives, swiftly and substantially, globally transforming lives, disrupting health, the economy, travel, and daily routines. The enormous change spared no area of our existence. From the grocery store showdowns over toilet paper, the infamous half-dressed Zoom meetings, or the made-up technological excuses, this global crisis undoubtedly changed everything, including the good ol' workplace. The pandemic's unique nature and global scale have made it a defining event of the 21st century, demanding adaptability, resilience, and collective action from individuals, communities, and governments worldwide, with some events bringing us laughs.

While the employees were split between the desire for interpersonal interaction for networking or gossip, and the unexpected ease of working from home and savings on dry-cleaning, businesses struggled with remote work. With the new exposure to Zoom meetings, bosses learned of their not-so-lighthearted evaluations from unmuted employees. Oops! Organizations trying to balance productivity, employee well-being, and the changing dynamics of the modern workplace face substantial problems.

Organizations have finally discovered the holy grail of work-life balance: the magical limits of flexible and hybrid work models. Who knew working remotely in your pajamas could be the ultimate game-changer? Now, business managers are scratching their heads, trying to evaluate the seismic shift in workplace culture. It's like a never-ending episode of Survivor: Office Edition, where the old workplace ideas are stranded in empty office space, trying to justify signed leases. Time to bid adieu to the old ways, swing both ways and embrace this new world of flexible work before the office becomes a relic of the past, like fax machines and beepers. Let's face this wave of uncertainty and loss with a smile, knowing that the future of work will embrace flexibility like a contortionist doing a pretzel-like pose.

And who needed pay-per-view when we witnessed politicians shutting, reopening businesses down, or throwing verbal jabs at doctors and scientists trying to stay afloat or save lives, respectively? We've witnessed comic book politicians confidently spewing medical advice like Dr. Seuss. From suggesting the ingestion of disinfectants to cure the virus (please, don't try this at home!) to promoting questionable miracle cures, their advice left us laughing or over one million dead. God bless the medical field for maintaining their composure and providing expert advice while dodging the curveballs thrown by politicians.

The idea that things will return to how they were before COVID is absurd. Employees mastered the art of working in their sweats, attending meetings with only blouses or shirts visible, or matching ensembles as your Covid-19 coworker, your pets. After learning about working remotely, employees will detest the thought of their entire workday incarcerated in the office.

The managers must be adaptable and sensibly decide with their superpowers. The epidemic has allowed businesses to rebuild their workplace culture because your returning employees have changed attitudes.

You don't want to mess this up and retrain and rehire new employees. It will be like trying to squeeze back into your high school jeans after years of indulging in fast food and takeout – it will work with magical creativity and consideration of the broader picture. Buckle up the blender of remote work and in-office collaboration. Create a workplace culture that feels like something other than a never-ending PowerPoint presentation to win over your remote-loving, pajama-wearing employees.

And employees, don't be too hard on your managers when you return. They're facing the daunting task of revamping the office and making it a place you want to be. Some will be oblivious, thinking it will all be the same. Those in the know, know they face the challenge of turning a haunted workplace into a staycation retreat - challenging but not impossible. So, let's join forces, managers and employees, colleague to colleague, and participate in a productive grind. For a short time, we might have to accept someone who comes into work wearing fluffy slippers or eating someone else's food from the snack room refrigerator mindlessly if they show a hint of productivity.

Most folks thrive on in-person social engagement and looking out to connect. But let's not leave out our fellow introverts who prefer blissful silence, undisturbed by outside noise or silence. They are like ninjas of direction, silently slaying tasks without external disturbances. Many looked forward to commuting from home to work daily to enjoy Monday morning coffee with coworkers, impromptu office conversations, and brainstorming sessions before the pandemic.

This abruptly ended as offices were closed, and employees began working remotely without having face-to-face meetings. Business leaders were concerned about their profits and expenses but also feared the threat of workplace culture. Has the old organizational culture suffered because of these changes creating a case of the jitters? It's like watching a drama unfold, with plot twists and suspense.

Picture the workplace situation as a buffet of possibilities, with various answers falling like the golden buzzard of America's Got Talent. Some remote employees are so done with months of solitude and social distancing that they're begging for a time machine to take them to what was. However, it's becoming as clear as day that many employees will regret a return to those old-school office restrictions. Remote work has unleashed a whole new world of perks. We're talking about the flexibility to work in your pajama bottoms, kiss those daily commutes goodbye, and embrace the sweetness of autonomy. It's like a revolution, a fundamental reevaluation of what the perfect workspace means.

Each person brings their own unique set of skills and quirks to the table. Some thrive in their cozy home caves, churning out work like productivity powerhouses, while others need the buzzing energy of face-to-face interactions to hit their stride. Working from home has unleashed a whole new dimension of connection and camaraderie. We've peered into the private lives of our bosses and colleagues, discovering their needy pets or home office screens while coincidently at the beach. This newfound insight has sparked empathy and humanity, like we're all part of one slightly dysfunctional family.

Workplace culture is about something other than being physically glued to the same office space or participating in trust falls during team-building exercises. Nope, it's all about fostering a caring and respectful mindset. Think of it as one large support blanket wrapped snugly around every employee. We may have shifted away from cutthroat competition and client obsession, but we've embraced a more empathetic approach to lifting each other.

Now, here's where it gets interesting. As these daring employees step into a brand-new workplace, they're met with a wave of apprehension. Some might even contemplate career changes, ready to swap spreadsheets for something more adventurous. Meanwhile, poor employers are scratching their heads, wondering how to navigate this hybrid workplace extravaganza, where remote work opportunities are as abundant as those fancy coffee flavors at the hipster café.

But keeping that workplace culture intact is crucial no matter where your team ends up—back in the office or surfing the small wave. It's like keeping a rare baseball card away safe, unlike in the attic of your aloof mom. So, managers, whether organizing socially distanced team-building activities or orchestrating virtual happy hours, understanding how your employees interact and keeping that spirit alive is the game's name.

Zen Navigation of Post-Pandemic Office Dynamics: Fight, Flight, or Fellowship offers helpful advice for businesses, leaders, and employees by taking an introspective journey into the tectonic office changes brought on by the pandemic. By emphasizing self-awareness, we aim to investigate methods for accepting workplace change, comprehending individual preferences, and establishing a culture of cooperation, trust, and respect. We will also look at the critical role of effective communication, emotional intelligence, and empathy in developing deep relationships among coworkers.

As we navigate the post-COVID era and learn how to establish a work atmosphere that welcomes change, celebrates diversity, and fosters a long-lasting sense of harmony and contentment, let's embrace the new normal, whether we're the social butterflies yearning for that office buzz or the introverts reveling in the sweet silence of solitude. Suppose we will accept ideas like healthy work environments and mindfulness. There, we'll create a whole new office culture filled with laughter, resilience, and an appreciation for the extroverts and the introverts among us. Let the workplace adventure begin!

The only way to do great work is to love what you do. - Dogen Zenji.

CHAPTER
ONE
EMBRACING THE NEW NORMAL

Be where you are; otherwise, you will miss your life. - Buddha

Covid came swinging in like a wrecking ball, but in the wise words of Selina Gomez and Rema, we all need to Calm Down. Consider it the theme song to your journey of self-discovery after lockdown. And hey, don't worry about feeling like a lone ranger on this adventure; we're all in this funky quest together!

Working from home has made us all a little soft. Our brains have forgotten how to focus in a noisy environment, and we've gotten used to taking our sweet time getting things done. Now that we're back in the office, we must re-learn how to work effectively around distractions.

But don't worry; it's not all bad news. Getting back into the swing of things can be fun! There's nothing like being surrounded by coworkers; social interaction can help us be more productive. So next time you're tempted to take a long lunch break or log off early, remember that it's all part of getting your brain back in shape.

Work was mostly connected to actual offices a few years back. There were few opportunities for remote work, and expectations were modest. However, the COVID-19 epidemic dramatically changed this environment, forcing a sizeable portion of the workforce to switch to remote work quickly. The future's course appears unpredictable and sluggish amid 2020's dramatic developments. But now it's time to burn those pajamas, store those pictures of your cuddling pets, and prepare for the gas prices and commute times.

There have been many attempts to predict the upcoming new normal, but given the importance of work in our lives, this cannot be determined until the future of work is investigated. A firm's chances of returning to work are less likely than two years ago because of the concurrent rise of vaccines and new varieties.

It takes more effort than simply unlocking office doors to resume regular workday activities. According to productivity experts' observations, establishing a new habit typically takes 21 days. Given this, significant obstacles remain after two years of remote employment. Reverting to one's pre-existing molds is impractical because so many people have moved, changed their careers, obtained higher education, and started or grown their families. Embracing the new office normal is like teaching an old fax machine a new trick. Instead of slapping on the new ordinary label, let's take a wild ride and liken the pandemic's impact to when the Industrial Revolution turned work into a whole new ballgame.

When we talk about the future of work, we talk about how our interactions with tasks at work, achieving goals, and balancing work and personal obligations are changing. Changes in social, economic, and global dynamics cause these modifications. While cultural changes are generally gradual, occasionally catalytic events cause unheard-of alterations.

Henry Ford's invention of the assembly line was a crucial historical trigger for changing work. The work week was reduced from 72 to 40 hours, revolutionizing working conditions while boosting productivity, employee well-being, and retention. Although a relatively recent creation, the 40-hour work week has become the norm in many businesses worldwide.

Traditional professional practices, such as actual offices, business travel, and formal clothes, disappeared between 2020 and 2021. The pandemic hastened the shift to a new type of work dynamic that, if adopted, can improve productivity, environmental sustainability, and work-life balance.

The workforce was divided into two categories—essential and non-essential—as the pandemic imposed social isolation. The former adopted technology to support distant work, while the latter maintained essential services like food distribution, transportation, and healthcare. Actors, fitness instructors, and food service employees are examples of professionals whose jobs required physical presence but lacked the flexibility to operate remotely.

Companies also had to deal with contradictions. While some companies struggled and had to switch to remote operations or temporarily close physical offices, others embraced remote work and managed the situation efficiently.

In contrast to businesses, employees found it more challenging to endure the pandemic's prolonged course. As unemployment benefits dried up and people struggled with desperation, many looked for new career paths or moved to more inexpensive areas. The Great Resignation phenomenon has caused businesses to struggle to return workers to their pre-pandemic lifestyles.

There were discussions about the effects of distant work on collaboration during the pandemic. Others across numerous sectors reported comparable or better productivity while working remotely, but some needed face-to-face connections. Starting a new job often entails face-to-face encounters. Still, the spread of work across time zones makes it difficult to form relationships, especially for members of Generation Z entering the workforce.

Employees in badly affected industries, including hospitality and food service, sought job changes to reclaim control amid lockdowns and constantly shifting laws. Because of the diminished job security, firms found it difficult to recruit employees. But industries with rapid expansion might provide incentives to deal with rising demand. These sectors either resisted automation or benefited from hybrid work arrangements.

The sustainability of such measures depends on industrial expansion, despite wage rises and improved benefits in lower-paying positions. Even while it was occasionally unavoidable, the termination of low-paying jobs due to the pandemic highlighted how vulnerable these positions were. After the epidemic, many workers may need to reskill and upgrade their skills to transition into booming businesses.

However, pursuing more salary is a challenging endeavor. Individuals may be discouraged from quickly seizing lucrative opportunities if they are still experiencing emotional pain from the pandemic. It takes energy, effort, and confidence to rethink a profession through job changes or creation; these traits may lack after years of uncertainty.

The workforce wants to change for the better. Thus, it needs assistance to overcome obstacles. Recognizing collective trauma is essential as the workplace landscape changes. The patterns of resignations serve as a constant reminder of the value of remote employment. Before the pandemic, several businesses had adopted remote work, with positive results. Beyond pandemic restrictions, remote labor is appealing because of its advantages across numerous industries.

Nevertheless, interpersonal relationships and teamwork continue regardless of the physical or virtual platform. An opportunity presents itself to create a unique workspace that serves both the needs of employees and customers. The secret is to embrace the transformative potential in the post-2020 whispers of change rather than trying to recreate the past. A shift toward a new normal that integrates work with personal fulfillment, purpose, clarity, passion, and equilibrium beckons.

Over the past thirty years, the nature of work has experienced a seismic transformation. The COVID-19 pandemic's rapid spread brought remote work to the fore and changed how traditional work dynamics function. This change has sparked discussions about how we will approach tasks, balance our personal and professional lives, and adjust to shifting economic and social paradigms. The pandemic-induced changes redefined what it meant to be at work, mirroring the effects of historical catalysts like Ford's assembly line.

The distinction between essential and non-essential occupations and businesses' responses becomes apparent as we consider this new workplace environment. Businesses must adjust to changing employment preferences and career trajectories, as seen by the Great Resignation phenomenon. While sectors experiencing growth take advantage of incentives and their particular suitability for hybrid models, those sectors experiencing disruption due to the pandemic need help to recruit workers back.

Emotional distress and collective trauma must be addressed to support the workforce and address the changing workplace environment. The continued popularity of remote work and the development of customized workspaces highlight the significance of balancing real-world and digital connections.

Ultimately, the future of employment depends on accepting change rather than returning to the status quo. Recognizing the opportunities offered by this paradigm shift and moving toward a new norm that prioritizes individual empowerment and comprehensive work experiences are where the transformative potential lies.

CHAPTER TWO
BEGIN WITH SELF-AWARENESS

Know well what leads you forward and what holds you back, and choose the path that leads to wisdom. - Buddha

Self-awareness is knowing yourself inside out, like an expert detective of your thoughts, emotions, and behaviors. It's like having a spotlight on your mind, shining a bright light on your strengths, weaknesses, and quirks. For example, when you catch yourself dancing like nobody's watching in the office kitchen, that's self-awareness! Or when you realize that you need that morning coffee to function at work, that's self-awareness! We want to add some depth to self-awareness.

Knowing yourself and understanding others are like two peas in a pod—these talents thrive on a dedicated tag team effort, unlike the bogus pro-wrestling entertainment. Self-awareness and social sensitivity are complementary skills that benefit from working together. Knowing oneself is essential to discovering one's way around the world. If we don't have enough empathy and compassion for ourselves, how can we give to and share it with others?

The development of self-awareness emerges as a crucial ability in the pursuit of improved well-being, more significant influence, improved decision-making abilities, and increased leadership effectiveness. Self-awareness is the foundation and primary muscle to develop to travel toward the most elevated version of oneself and the most skilled leadership embodiment possible.

Healing, evolving, and transforming the world sounds challenging, but guess what? It all starts with you! That's right, you're the star of this show, and it's all about self-awareness. Recently, this buzzword's been popping up everywhere, especially around the office water cooler. It's like the hottest trend in management and leadership, and why not? Knowing yourself – feelings, thoughts, strengths, and weaknesses – is like having a magical guide to career growth. It's your very own You for Smarties handbook!

Now, let's dive into what self-awareness means. Picture yourself at the captain's wheel of a ship called Emotional Intelligence. Understanding your feelings and thoughts is like having the fanciest navigation system. You can steer through daily decisions like a pro, all while looking fabulous doing it. So next time you're faced with a choice, tap into your inner awesomeness, and watch the magic happen!

Social awareness is like having a magical empathy wand that helps you understand and connect with the feelings of others. It's like having a radar for the emotions of your coworkers, knowing when they need a pick-me-up or when they're ready to conquer the world. For example, when you notice your colleague is feeling down and bring them a slice of cake because you know it's their comfort food, that's social awareness. Or when you sense that your teammate needs some space after a tough meeting, that's social awareness.

A person who has mastered self-awareness can better evaluate themselves, control their emotions, align their behavior with their morals, and perceive others' perceptions effectively. Self-awareness training is imperative since it equips people with commitment skills to assess their development and change course.

The internal and the external commitments are two keys intertwined yet separate elements and form the foundation of self-awareness. Self-awareness develops internally as the path to personal fulfillment through the complex landscapes of aspirations, feelings, thoughts, and perceptions. External commitments promote greater community satisfaction among your peers in the face of difficulty. It is an investigation into the area of popular consciousness, probing how those around them view one. A person who can align their actions with this dimension can inspire trust among their team members and, in doing so, elevates themselves to the pinnacle of understanding and empathy.

Our lives are like a dance routine with two interconnected moves: self-awareness and social awareness. These pillars lay the foundation for emotional intelligence, allowing us to bust out killer moves on balance, resilience, creativity, cooperation, and inventiveness. This chapter will show how self-awareness can turn your work environment into a happy space.

Post-COVID office dynamics can be a wild rollercoaster ride of emotions with unexpected twists and turns, from the excitement of reuniting with colleagues to the fear of uncertainty about the future. For instance, one moment, you're feeling ecstatic because the team nailed a project, and the next moment, you're anxious about the ever-changing work policies. It can be a mix of emotions with thrilling highs and nerve-wracking lows.

It's not me is a common thought because most everyone thinks they're the best behind the wheel, and most of us think we are self-aware, but the reality is quite the opposite. It's like being a fantastic driver on a road trip in middle America and facing your first day in New York City or Los Angeles traffic.

We are at a crossroads of introspection and observation in the world of self-awareness. In this crazy rollercoaster ride of post-COVID office dynamics, being mindful of self-awareness is like having a safety harness that keeps you grounded and secure. Self-awareness helps you navigate through the highs and lows with grace and resilience. When mindful of your emotions and reactions, you can avoid emotional derailments and communicate effectively with your team. So, buckle up, embrace self-awareness, and enjoy the exhilarating ride of post-COVID office dynamics!

BENEFITS

The numerous benefits of fostering self-awareness are as varied as the people themselves. The benefits of knowing oneself are sweet. These benefits include greater perspective, more impact, and deeper connections. Let's explore the complex web of self-awareness, clarifying its meaning, defining its boundaries, and outlining strategies to promote its development.

Imagine having Improved Emotional Intelligence, self-assurance, and originality, making better decisions and Problem-Solving, enhanced communication and Conflict Resolution, Building Resilience and Coping with Change improving your relationships, and becoming a more effective leader. Internal self-awareness is about knowing our deepest desires, feelings, ideas, values, strengths, and even our quirky flaws (because we all have them!). Meanwhile, being aware of how others see and react to us is a benefit and power. Despite all the information from psychologists and academics, there still needs to be a chasm of difference between theory and consciously honing this skill.

There is no sudden flash of insight or a toggle switch for awareness. It's more of a spectrum, a scale on which levels of self-awareness can be found. At other times, we're as disconnected from ourselves as your friend who gets lost even when sober. Being self-aware entails being mindful of one's internal and external mental processes and emotional and behavioral responses to the zany world around one.

Self-awareness helps control your emotions. When you know your emotions like the back of your hand, you become an emotional Jedi. You won't fly off the handle when Bob from accounting eats your lunch (again!), and you'll have the wisdom to pat yourself when you ace that presentation.

Having insight into your skills gives you more self-assurance: Picture yourself walking into the office like a boss! When you're self-aware, you radiate confidence. You won't second-guess your abilities when tackling new challenges, and you'll rock that critical client meeting with committed confidence.

An in-depth look into self-awareness allows you to appreciate your originality. Your originality allows a creative spark that sets your ideas on fire. You won't be a cookie-cutter employee but a unicorn in a land of mules. Embrace your quirks and your uniqueness. There is no other you in this world, even if you are a twin.

When you are self-aware of your assessments, you make better decisions. No more flipping coins or asking your dog if she wants to go for a walk. There's no decision paralysis because you trust your instincts and your assets. You'll weigh your options like a pro and make choices that align with your values and goals.

Self-awareness helps you sleuth through problems like Sherlock Holmes on a mission. You'll spot patterns and connections and develop innovative solutions to solve problems.

You can express yourself with clarity and empathy, thus enhancing communication. Self-awareness is like a language translator for your emotions. You'll be confident about what you can do and need to work on.

Self-awareness is like a peace treaty between your emotions and rationality, so you will be better positioned to resolve conflict. You can learn to handle conflicts like a diplomat and reduce office drama as a peacemaker by respecting others, finding common ground, and understanding others' perspectives.

Building resilience comes with self-awareness. You'll bounce back from setbacks and face challenges with a can-do attitude. Adversity will be a bumpy road on your path to success!

Self-awareness allows you to cope with and manage change. You won't fear the unknown; instead, you'll embrace change with adventure. Transitions will be acceptable, whether high or low.

By spending time on in-depth self-awareness, your relationships will improve. You'll build deeper connections with others as you know whom to hang with and who to avoid. You'll know when to lend a listening ear or offer a helping hand, and your relationships and attitude will bloom.

And no matter your position or station in life, your path to self-awareness begins with a purpose to better yourself. That means you will be a more effective leader or team leader. Your authenticity and emotional intelligence will make you a leader worth following.

In the Zen garden of the mind, where thoughts and feelings flow like a gentle stream, mastering self-awareness is akin to understanding the ripples and currents of one's inner landscape. To know oneself is to walk in harmony with emotions, aligning each step with one's most profound morals and perceiving the world through clear, compassionate eyes. The practice of self-awareness becomes a tranquil journey, a path where commitment and reflection guide us likewise old trees, helping us evaluate our growth and gently change our course when needed.

Consider the delicate balance of the internal and external commitments—two elements, distinct yet interwoven like the yin and yang, forming the very foundation of self-awareness. Internally, we navigate the complex landscapes of our dreams, emotions, and perceptions, seeking personal fulfillment as effortlessly as a leaf floats on water. Externally, we cultivate connections and trust, probing the reflections in the pond of collective consciousness. This alignment with others is like a gentle breeze, inspiring trust within a community and elevating oneself to the peak of understanding and empathy. In this delicate dance of inner and outer awareness, one finds a serene and enlightened path, a Zen way to navigate the complexities of being human.

SELF-AWARENESS PROCESS

How can we develop a more profound sense of who we are? We have many methods at our disposal. Let's think more gently of one another, lighten ourselves up, and accept our flaws and eccentricities. We can keep our feet firmly on the ground, be open to hearing the perspectives of others (they probably have great anecdotes to share), and be comfortable enough with ourselves to recognize our shortcomings and actively seek to rectify them. Finding the optimal rate to navigate self-awareness is as easy as adjusting the dimmer on a ceiling fan.

Let's start with the professional organizations that assess behavior and personalities. We will review the Myers-Briggs test more, but others assess extraversion, agreeableness, openness, conscientiousness, or neuroticism.

DISC Assessment measures four dimensions of behavior: Dominance, Influence, Steadiness, and Compliance. Enneagram Test evaluates nine personality types, each with its own unique set of motivations and values. StrengthsFinder judges 34 strengths, which can identify your natural talents and abilities. 16 Personalities measures 16 personality types, each with its own unique set of preferences and traits. Keirsey Temperament Sorter evaluates four temperaments: Artisan, Guardian, Idealist, and Rational. And, The Color Code analyses four personality types: Red, Blue, White, and Yellow.

The Myers-Briggs Type Indicator (MBTI) is a personality evaluation instrument that offers insightful information about a person's preferences, skills, and weaknesses. The sixteen personality types identified by the MBTI are based on Carl Jung's notion of psychological types.

The MBTI gauges four main personality traits:

The difference between extraversion (E) and introversion (I) indicates whether a person gets their energy from the outside world (extraverts) or the inside (introverts).

Information gathering is related to this dimension, which contrasts sensing (S) with intuition (N). While intuitive types concentrate on patterns and possibilities, sensing types depend on specific facts and specifics.

The thinking vs. feeling dimension describes how people make choices. While feeling types consider the influence on people's emotions and values, thinking types stress reason and objective analysis.

This dimension contrasts how people see and judge the outer world (J vs. P). Perceiving types are malleable, flexible, and open to new possibilities, whereas judging types want structure, order, and closure.

The Myers-Briggs Type Indicator (MBTI) is a valuable resource for individuals to understand themselves and others better. Knowing their personality type, they can identify their preferred communication style, problem-solving approach, and ideal work setting. Extroverts thrive in social and collaborative environments, while introverts excel in quieter and contemplative situations.

The MBTI sheds light on how personality types influence interpersonal interactions. Recognizing preferences allows people to adjust their communication style and build stronger connections with others. This knowledge fosters efficient teamwork, empathy, and mutual respect in the workplace.

The MBTI enables individuals to assess their strengths and weaknesses objectively. Understanding their talents empowers them to utilize their skills effectively and contribute efficiently to the team. Similarly, identifying areas for improvement motivates people to grow and develop. So, take a professional test early to set you on your path.

The author regrets not following the early and frequent advice of journaling daily events. Reflection and journaling are potent methods of self-awareness that allow individuals to gain deeper insights into their thoughts, emotions, and behaviors. Taking time for self-reflection helps to understand the reasons behind specific actions and reactions. Keeping a journal provides a safe space to express feelings and experiences, helping to identify patterns and triggers. For example, by reflecting on a challenging interaction with a colleague, someone might realize that a fear of criticism drove their defensive response. They can explore ways to address this fear and respond constructively through journaling. Seriously, start and follow through with consistency. And make sure your journals are legible. You may know what you wrote that day, but returning to your notes may be as complex as reading a doctor's prescription.

Seeking feedback from others and listening to their perspectives can be eye-opening for self-awareness. Constructive feedback from colleagues, friends, or mentors can shed light on blind spots and areas for improvement. Listening to others' feedback requires an open mind and a willingness to consider different viewpoints. For instance, during a performance review, employee feedback about their communication style makes them realize that they dominate conversations. They can communicate more inclusively by listening and reflecting on this feedback. NOTE: No one is consistent. Someone getting an exceptional performance rating may not perform the same the next period, which means you too. We see that through athletes and biorhythms.

Mindfulness and meditation cultivate present-moment awareness and a non-judgmental attitude. Mindfulness involves paying attention to thoughts, emotions, and sensations as they arise without getting caught up in them. Meditation helps to train the mind and develop focus and clarity. By practicing mindfulness and meditation regularly, individuals become more attuned to their thoughts and reactions, allowing them to recognize automatic patterns and respond more intentionally. For example, during a mindfulness session, someone might notice anxiety about an upcoming presentation and use grounding techniques to reduce stress. Start with baby steps because time is an excuse.

Recognizing and addressing unconscious biases and assumptions is crucial for self-awareness. We all have biases and discriminate when we make simple choices on food, attire, or personalities. Unconscious biases are deeply ingrained attitudes that influence how we perceive and interact with others. By learning of these biases, individuals can strive to treat all team members fairly and equally. For example, a manager might realize that they assign specific tasks based on gender and work on distributing responsibilities more objectively.

Understanding personal triggers and emotional reactions is essential for managing conflicts and stress effectively. Individuals can develop coping strategies and better control their reactions by recognizing what situations provoke strong emotional responses. For instance, an employee might notice that receiving critical feedback triggers feelings of defensiveness, and they can then work on responding constructively. Be the bigger person.

Limiting beliefs are self-imposed mental barriers that hinder personal growth and success. We all have them through family, friends, or location. Self-awareness allows individuals to identify these limiting beliefs and challenge them. For example, an individual may believe they need to be more skilled for a promotion. Still, through self-awareness, they can recognize their accomplishments and potential, allowing them to pursue advancement opportunities.

Self-awareness is vital in building positive relationships and fostering colleague trust. By understanding their communication styles and emotional triggers, individuals can interact more effectively with others. For instance, team members who know they are impatient in meetings can actively work on listening more attentively to their colleagues' ideas. This self-awareness helps create an open communication environment where team members feel heard and valued, strengthening relationships and increasing trust.

Office dynamics can sometimes lead to challenging situations and conflicts. Self-awareness enables individuals to respond to such situations with emotional intelligence. Recognizing their emotions and triggers empowers them to stay calm and composed during disagreements. For example, a manager aware that they become defensive when receiving criticism can practice self-regulation to respond more constructively and empathetically. Handling difficult situations with emotional intelligence promotes a healthier work environment and strengthens working relationships.

Fostering Inclusivity and Empathy: Self-awareness enhances inclusivity and empathy within the office environment. By understanding their biases and assumptions, individuals can challenge and overcome them. This opens the door for embracing diversity and creating a culture of inclusivity. For instance, an employee who recognizes their unconscious bias towards a particular gender may actively work on treating all team members equally and providing equal opportunities. This fosters an atmosphere of empathy and appreciation for everyone's unique perspectives, resulting in increased collaboration and creativity.

Self-awareness contributes to the promotion of a supportive and collaborative culture within the office. By being mindful of their strengths and limitations, individuals can seek assistance and offer help to their colleagues when possible. For example, an employee who knows they excel in problem-solving can volunteer to assist a coworker facing a challenging task. This collaborative spirit creates a sense of unity and teamwork, leading to increased productivity and a positive work environment.

Self-awareness plays a crucial role in overcoming challenges and developing resilience in adversity. By being aware of their strengths and limitations, individuals can approach challenges with a growth mindset and a positive attitude. For example, an employee who faces a setback on a project can reflect on their mistakes, learn from them, and develop a new approach. This self-awareness empowers them to bounce back more robust and determined, fostering a sense of resilience that helps them confidently tackle future challenges.

Self-awareness enables individuals to handle resistance and adapt to change more effectively. By recognizing their emotional reactions to change, individuals can respond with emotional intelligence, allowing them to navigate through transitions smoothly. For instance, a manager aware of their resistance to change can work on embracing new ideas and encouraging their team to do the same. This creates a more adaptable and flexible work environment where individuals can thrive amidst changing circumstances.

Self-awareness encourages self-compassion and self-care. Individuals can prioritize self-care practices that boost their resilience and mental health by understanding their emotional needs and well-being. For example, an employee aware of feeling burnt out can take a day off to rest and recharge, promoting a healthier work-life balance. This self-awareness fosters a caring culture for oneself and one another, creating a supportive workplace where employees can thrive.

Self-awareness helps individuals find a balance between work and personal life. Individuals can take proactive measures to maintain a healthy balance by recognizing signs of stress or burnout. For instance, team members who know they overwork can set boundaries and establish a time for personal hobbies and activities. This self-awareness fosters a positive work environment where employees feel encouraged to prioritize their well-being and enjoy a fulfilling personal life outside of work.

Cultivating a self-awareness mindset involves seeking to understand oneself and being open to personal growth. For example, employees might regularly reflect and journal to gain insights into their thoughts and emotions. They may also practice mindfulness and meditation to stay present and in tune with their feelings. By adopting this mindset, individuals can become more in touch with their strengths and areas for improvement, leading to greater self-awareness and personal development.

As a leader, encouraging self-awareness among team members is essential for fostering a harmonious and high-performing team. Leaders can create a safe and supportive environment where team members feel comfortable sharing their thoughts and emotions. For instance, during team meetings, leaders can encourage open discussions about individual strengths and weaknesses and opportunities for growth. By promoting a culture of self-awareness, team members are more likely to communicate effectively, understand each other's perspectives, and collaborate more efficiently.

Embracing Vulnerability and Growth: Leaders can inspire self-awareness among their team members by leading by example. Embracing vulnerability and openly discussing their growth journey can encourage others to do the same. For example, a manager might share a personal experience of overcoming a professional challenge and the valuable lessons learned from it. By demonstrating vulnerability and a commitment to growth, leaders create a culture where mistakes are viewed as opportunities for learning and self-improvement.

Embracing mistakes and learning from failures is a crucial aspect of self-awareness. When individuals acknowledge and take responsibility for their errors, they foster a culture of accountability and continuous improvement. For instance, a team member who makes a mistake on a project can admit to it during a team meeting and discuss how they plan to rectify the situation. By doing so, they demonstrate self-awareness and a willingness to learn from their failures, which can inspire others to do the same.

You may have noticed a severe tone in self-awareness compared to the beginning of the chapter. Self-awareness requires a severe effort for growth. It is work! It is the foundation for personal and professional growth. By embracing your authentic self and cultivating a self-awareness mindset, you can navigate post-COVID office dynamics with confidence and emotional intelligence. Self-awareness allows you to understand your strengths and weaknesses, recognize your emotional reactions, and build positive relationships with your colleagues. Make the process a commitment and habit. It may take more of your time at the beginning. However, habits will take less time for you to enjoy the benefits this world offers.

You can gain valuable insights into your thoughts, feelings, and behaviors through reflection, journaling, seeking feedback, and practicing mindfulness. Embracing vulnerability and acceptance enables you to be open to personal growth and learn from mistakes and failures. By recognizing blind spots, unconscious biases, and limiting beliefs, you can overcome challenges and stay resilient in the face of resistance and change.

As the person you are now, encouraging self-awareness among your team members creates a supportive and collaborative culture where everyone feels valued and understood. Leading by example and embracing vulnerability can inspire your team to do the same. By empowering your journey to self-awareness, you become a more effective and empathetic leader, guiding your team toward success in the post-COVID workplace.

Navigating post-COVID office dynamics with confidence and emotional intelligence requires a deep understanding of oneself and others. By embracing self-awareness, you can build positive relationships, handle difficult situations gracefully, foster inclusivity and empathy, and promote a supportive and collaborative work environment. With self-awareness as your compass, you can thrive in the ever-evolving workplace and create a fulfilling and successful career journey. So, embark on self-discovery, and watch as self-awareness transforms your work life and your entire being.

JOURNEY

In the quiet garden of the mind, ask yourself soul-stirring questions. Like a gentle breeze, let the answers come to you: Do your values dance harmoniously with your actions? What strengths bloom within you, and what limitations hide in the shadows? In Zen, every answer leads to a new question; thus, understanding oneself becomes a beautiful, endless cycle.

Begin with a single step, a sincere look into the soul's mirror. Embrace feedback as a wise friend who reveals the hidden treasures within you. Let mindfulness be your dance partner, moving gracefully with the world around you. In the tranquil pond of consciousness, every ripple tells a story.

Self-awareness is not a destination but a gentle, winding path, a soft lantern guiding you through the labyrinth of life. It must flow like water, adapting and changing as life does. How will you sail toward your enlightened self today? This question, a compass of wisdom, leads you to the best version of yourself.

See self-awareness as a lantern, casting a soft glow on the path to well-being, leadership, and refined decision-making. Like a finely tuned instrument, this transformative ability resonates with the melody of your potential. Pursuing self-awareness becomes an art, a symphony of introspection, questions, feedback, and mindfulness. The valid reward, more than mere self-discovery, is creating a path rich with meaning, growth, and fulfillment.

Step through your mind and follow up with one action each day. In the calm embrace of Zen, may you find your way, one mindful step at a time.

CHAPTER
THREE
OFFICE PERSONALITIES

To see a person's true nature, look not at their words but at their actions. - Lao Tzu

We're back in the office after what feels like a thousand Zoom calls in our sweatpants! So, gather the gang because it's time to decode the newly adjusted personalities in our workplace. It's like having a real-life episode of The Office. So, grab your favorite mug, settle into your moldy reclaimed office chair, and dive into the world of office personalities. Let's make the most of the post-COVID office experience.

Collaboration is like trying to make a fantastic Jambalaya in the office jungle. You've got your leadership crawfish leading the way, the sensible shrimps keeping things rational, and a quirky crab occasionally throwing in a different flavor. We must also mix and match andouille with various seasonings to savor the deliciousness of each team's project.

Workplace personality types encompass behavioral patterns in formal situations. While some prefer to focus on and complete tasks thoroughly, others are better at delegating and energizing a team. While closely associated with traditional personality categories, these workplace personality types stand out due to their significant effects on workplace performance dynamics.

When you put competing work personalities together, things can get, let's say, interesting, like trying to mix oil with water. But mastering the art of understanding these workplace 'flavors' is more straightforward than whipping up a quick breakfast. We'll share secret recipes on waltzing with opposite personality types and tips on sprinkling chameleon charm into your persona.

Recognizing the many personality types present in a team is crucial, whether you're an employer or an employee. This information enhances collaborative synergy by enabling effective teamwork among individuals with disparate personality qualities. Employers are better equipped, thanks to this understanding to maximize each team member's contribution, promoting better mental health and job satisfaction.

Many personality types show up in and out of the job. Each person possesses particular advantages and disadvantages. Even with limited resources, combining these strengths can support the completion of challenging undertakings.

You know there's always one person in the office who is perpetually late and seems to live in their time zone. That's just one personality of many we'll be decoding in this chapter. We'll start with the Leader.

The Leader personality type is a pillar of the corporate environment and coordinates the concerted pursuit of shared goals. They strive to be executives. While analytical thinking and creativity may differ from their strong suits, leaders are excellent at organizing effective processes. However, their unwavering attention to long-term objectives may cause them to become less alert to urgent creative visions. For this personality type, effective communication is essential.

The Leaders steer the ship and make sure we're all on the same page. Yet one Leader may be pumped to have us all back in person, while others might secretly miss their pajama-clad eye-gunk team meetings.

Collaborating with the Leader is all about being on the same wavelength. Well, when in the office, follow the Leader's lead! Whether they want daily check-ins or weekly brainstorming sessions, it's essential to show them that you're ready to support their vision even if they are rusty and more in touch with their cat during the lockdown and are now experiencing separation anxiety. So, be patient and understanding with them.

Then there is the workaholic go-getter who shows up bright-eyed and bushy-tailed, ready to conquer the world. Embrace their drive and let it motivate you to kickstart your day. Workaholics try to outdo their productivity record. They're like a tornado of productivity, and there's no stopping them. Challenge them, and they only work harder. They are risk-takers that excel in fast-paced environments. They can produce exceptional outcomes to foster an innovative spirit in a structured atmosphere.

Then there is the homeaholic who wants to avoid returning to the office and who's been living their best life in their home office. They've mastered the art of Zoom meetings and have their coffee mugs within arm's reach. These homeaholics are not thrilled about leaving the comfort of their nest and facing the dreaded commute. They must trade in their furry slippers for uncomfortable heels. All they need is a little office camaraderie to brighten their day. Let them know of the office perks – a few drops left in the coffee pot, the office gossip, or sharing a good laugh with your colleagues and realizing that being together makes the office unique. Remember that the office is a place for laughter, camaraderie, hilarious moments, and production.

We must include creative geniuses. They have colorful Post-it notes all over their workspace, a collection of quirky desk toys, and a dreamy look in their eyes, like they have solved the Rubik's Cube with their eyes closed. The creative is like a walking art exhibit, always ready to challenge the status quo and think outside the box. They're the ones who claim they get paid for what they know, not what they do. Dealing with this imaginative whirlwind might seem like a wild ride, but embrace the creative's unique perspective and let them inspire you to see things differently. The creative can sometimes get lost in their world of ideas.

They're like a balloon floating away, and it's your job to gently pull them back to reality. They may be funny and ready to crack a joke or two.

Those with analytical minds roam free, armed with spreadsheets and data galore. They love crunching data and analyzing every little detail. Ask for help, and they'll present you with a 10-page report with charts and graphs. But beware, because the analytical can also be the office detectives, meddling in everyone's affairs with their keen sense of observation. They can tell you who ate the last slice of pizza in the breakroom or two minutes late to the morning meeting. They have a sixth sense of office gossip and are unafraid to use it. On the bright side, analytical minds are fantastic problem solvers. They can dissect a complex issue and devise a solution no one else would have thought of. So, when you're stuck in a rut, turn to the analytical, and they'll have you out of it quickly.

The Analyst, mirroring the stillness of a deep pond, often seeks solitude, momentarily letting the ripples of others fade away. Yet, such stillness can sometimes cloud office harmony in a collective endeavor. The Analyst becomes a vessel of profound insight, gazing deeply into the project's puzzles and weaving solutions from the truth. But like a seasoned master recognizing the value of every student, the Analyst must also learn to embrace the office voices, lest their wisdom overshadows collective insight.

The Logician thrives on challenging intellectual tasks. Logicians frequently show introverted inclinations and prefer problems they can focus on. This contemplation may occasionally hamper their ability to read social cues. Despite this, the team dynamics benefit significantly from their presence. The Logician and the Logistician are similar, but the latter sets itself apart by adhering rigidly to rules and deadlines. This personality type excels at upholding team discipline and ensuring task alignment with deadlines. Working with logisticians requires a dedication to meeting deadlines, articulating duties, and meeting expectations.

The social butterfly has returned to the office, ready to spread their wings and renew friendships. These office socialites are like walking party planners, always organizing the next team lunch or happy hour. They've got a gift for building rapport with everyone they meet, and you can always count on them to break the ice in any awkward situation. The social butterfly is a master networker. They can introduce you to people you never knew existed and open doors you never thought possible. You might find them chatting away at the water cooler while a pile of papers sits untouched on their desk. Ultimately, the social butterfly brings a vibrant energy to the office that can't be replicated. They make work feel like a social gathering, making the office lively.

But be warned, because the social butterfly is also the office gossip. They've got their ear to the ground and know everyone's business, from who's dating whom to who got a promotion (and who didn't). They're like office news reporters, always in the know and ready to share the latest scoop. So, be careful what you share with them. They might seem like your best friend, but remember that anything you say could end up as office fodder. It's like living in a real-life soap opera, where the office analyzes and discusses every word and action.

As you return to the office after COVID-19, you'll be glad to have some team players on your side. These people are always willing to help, even doing something they don't want. They're always the first to volunteer for the less glamorous tasks and always willing to pick up the slack when someone else struggles.

The team player is the person who volunteers to be the designated driver after happy hour, brings snacks to meetings, or takes the blame for the team's mistakes. Team players are also essential for fostering collaboration and conflict resolution. They're the people able to bring different viewpoints together and find common ground. They're also able to mediate disagreements and help the team move forward. They're able to listen to each other's concerns, and they're willing to compromise. One of the most essential qualities of a team player is covering your back when you're not looking. They have a sixth sense of spotting when a coworker is struggling and are always willing to lend a helping hand, even if it means taking on extra work.

Let's not forget the perfectionists. These always strive for excellence, even if it means driving themselves crazy. They're the ones who will spend hours polishing a presentation no one will ever see or who will rewrite a report three times before they're satisfied. Perfectionism can be a great asset in the workplace. It can help you produce high-quality work and meet deadlines. However, find a balance between excellence and efficiency. If you're too focused on perfection, you can waste time and energy.

There's nothing wrong with striving for excellence. But sometimes, perfectionism can hinder productivity. Perfectionists can be so focused on perfection that they forget to finish things. They can also be overly critical of themselves and others, creating a stressful work environment. Perfectionists can be valuable assets in the workplace. Perfectionism is the art of never being satisfied and needing more time to do something half-assed. A perfectionist would rather be perfect than finished.

Ah, the Introvert, the master of quietly getting things done. They're like the stealth ninjas of the office, silently working their magic behind the scenes. While everyone else is busy chatting and brainstorming, the introvert huddles in their corner, coming up with brilliant ideas and strategies. They know the right amount of peace needed to foster productivity. While the extroverts are busy holding impromptu meetings in the hallway, the Introvert turns out their work in their zone.

Ultimately, the Introvert is the silent force that keeps the office balanced and harmonious. They may not be the life of the party or the loudest person in the room, but they sure know how to make the office function. The Introvert might not be, but their opinions and ideas carry weight.

The Campaigning Advocates are charismatic figures who shine in various social settings. Their skill in establishing rapport can be a huge advantage. But occasionally, this gregariousness turns into distractibility. To realize their potential, they must use their creativity while remaining focused. They are crucial allies for essential goals because of their dedication to causes and ideologies. Their fidelity and commitment are extraordinary. Protecting their privacy while putting them on relevant initiatives if you want to increase their engagement is crucial.

Caretakers are the mother hens. They're like a warm, fuzzy blanket, ready to comfort and support their coworkers. While everyone else is busy with deadlines and meetings, the caretaker ensures that everyone is comfortable. When someone is having a bad hair day, when they think they can't take anymore, the caretaker appears with a plate of cookies, a shot of tequila, or a joint. They have a sixth sense of knowing when someone needs a little extra TLC.

The caretaker is like the office therapist, always ready to lend a listening ear and offer encouragement. The caretaker is the glue that holds the office together, ensuring everyone feels valued and supported. They might not be the loudest person in the room, but everyone feels their presence. They might accidentally sign everyone up for a yoga or a triathlon, thinking it's a great way to de-stress. They may not be the CEO, but they know how to create a workplace that feels like a big warm hug.

And last but not least is Danny or Debbie Downer. Mentioning their names paints a picture. They throw a monkey wrench into topics and issues. They meddle in and debate politics, religion, and work products. They affect moods. Like a yawn or a smile, emotions are contagious. A constant negativity from a Downer can pull down the team's overall mood, making the atmosphere heavier and less energized. They can create decreased productivity and derail innovative ideas.

They shy from collaboration leading to fragmented team dynamics and increased stress. While a cautious approach to challenges can be beneficial, perpetual pessimism can prevent teams from finding solutions, focusing only on potential pitfalls. Downers can contribute to office attrition and strain leadership. Teams and leadership must proactively address these challenges through open communication, counseling, or training to maintain a healthy, positive work environment.

Learning to adjust to office personalities is essential. Expect people returning to the office to have changed, with many reluctant to spend 40 hours a week in an office setting.

FELLOWSHIP

Here are some office post-pandemic issues that may arise between some office personalities upon their return:

The Leader may have a challenge in managing the work-life balance of the Workaholic. They might need help convincing this employee to take breaks and avoid burnout, as they are constantly driven to work and achieve more. The Leader can have open and honest conversations with the workaholic go-getter about maintaining a healthy work-life balance. They can encourage the employee to take regular breaks and vacations to recharge. Offering flexible work arrangements and promoting wellness programs in the office can also help address this issue.

The Leader may need more support from the Homeaholic in returning to the office, as they have become accustomed to the comforts of working from home's comfy couch. They must be more confident about commuting, dressing up, and adhering to office schedules. The Leader can address this issue by gradually returning the Homeaholic to the office. They can start with a few days of in-office work and gradually increase the frequency. Providing a comfortable and flexible workspace can also help move smoother. Additionally, the Leader can highlight the benefits of in-person collaboration and the office environment's social interactions.

The Leader may encounter challenges in managing the Creative's unique perspective and approach to work. They might struggle to align the employee's innovative ideas with the organization's goals and processes. The Leader can foster an environment that encourages creativity and innovation while setting clear expectations and goals for the creative. They can create brainstorming sessions and idea-sharing opportunities, ensuring the employee's Creative input is valued. Additionally, the Leader can assign projects allowing the Creative to utilize their innovative skills while contributing to the organization's objectives.

The Leader may face difficulty managing the tendency of the Analytical to meddle in everyone's affairs and over-analyze situations. This could lead to communication breakdown and conflicts among team members. The Leader can help channel Analytical problem-solving skills by assigning tasks requiring analytical thinking and decision-making. They can also encourage the Analytical to focus on their tasks and provide constructive feedback to team members rather than getting overly involved in their affairs. Implementing clear communication protocols and team-building activities can foster better understanding and collaboration.

The Leader may need to address the Social Butterfly's habit of advising everyone on their business and being excessively involved in office affairs. This behavior could create distractions and misunderstandings among team members. The Leader can recognize and appreciate the Social Butterfly's networking skills while gently guiding them to focus on their tasks. They can set boundaries for office interactions and encourage more structured communication channels. Regular team meetings can ensure that important information is shared in a structured manner, avoiding unnecessary distractions.

The Leader may need to manage the Team Player's willingness to help, even when it means taking on too much and neglecting their tasks. The Leader can appreciate and acknowledge the Team Player's dedication while ensuring they don't become overwhelmed. They can encourage employees to communicate openly about their workload and set priorities. Delegating tasks effectively and recognizing the Team Player's efforts can help balance teamwork and individual responsibilities.

The Leader may need help creating a comfortable and inclusive work environment for the Introvert, as they may be more reserved and less likely to participate in group discussions. The Leader can create opportunities for one-on-one interactions with the Introverts, allowing them to express their ideas and concerns in a more comfortable setting. Providing platforms for written communication, such as emails or messaging apps, can also help Introverts share their thoughts and contribute to team discussions. Additionally, recognizing and celebrating individual achievements can help the Introvert feel valued and included in the office culture.

Creative vs. Analytical: The creative person may be annoyed by the analytical person's need for details, while the analytical person may feel like the creative person is not being practical. The creative person could try to be more open to the analytical person's need for details and could explain why they need some freedom to be creative. The analytical person could try to be more understanding of the creative person's need for freedom and could trust they will still produce high-quality work.

Social Butterfly vs. Introvert: The social butterfly may be annoyed by the Introvert's need for alone time, while the Introvert may feel like the social butterfly is too demanding of their attention. The social butterfly could try to respect the Introvert's need for alone time and find other ways to socialize, such as going out for lunch or coffee with colleagues. The Introverts could try to be more social and get to know their colleagues better.

Team Player vs. Workaholic: The team player may be annoyed by the Workaholic's need to work long hours, while the workaholic may feel like the team player is not pulling their weight. The team player could try to understand why the Workaholic feels the need to work long hours and could offer to help them reduce their workload. The Workaholic could try to be more mindful of their time and could learn to delegate tasks to others.

The Homeaholic and the Workaholic: Issue: The Homeaholic enjoys remote work, but the Workaholic believes productivity is higher in the office. The Homeaholic can show the Workaholic the benefits of remote work, like avoiding traffic and working in PJs. The Workaholic can appreciate the Homeaholic's preference and find a balance that benefits both productivity and preferences.

In this chapter about office personalities, we explored the personalities that make up the office dynamic. From the Leader to the caretaker, each contributes to the success of the post-COVID office dynamics uniquely, bringing humor and charm to the workplace.

Everyone is different, and there is no one-size-fits-all solution. The best way to resolve them is to communicate openly and honestly with each other and to be willing to compromise.

The Workaholic might need help understanding the Introvert's need for solitude and may perceive their reserved nature as a lack of enthusiasm. The Workaholic can recognize the Introvert's strengths in focused work and thoughtful contributions. The Leader can provide opportunities for the Introverts to express their ideas in ways that suit their comfort level, such as through written communication or one-on-one discussions. Creating an inclusive and supportive work environment can help The Introvert feel valued and understood. Everyone is different, and there is no one-size-fits-all solution. The best way to resolve them is to communicate openly and honestly with each other and to be willing to compromise.

PERSONALITY GOALS

Every soul is a unique blossom, each with its size, color, and fragrance. To nurture this garden, the wise gardener comprehends the essence of each bloom, knowing that light and shadow vary with each petal. When the gardener nurtures the potential of each blossom, the garden's hidden treasures awaken, and every plant flourishes.

Each blossom carries within them a tale of strengths and soft spots. As the gentle guide of these souls, you must lead and harmonize, allowing each petal to reach its potential in harmony, where wisdom lies in the delicate art of listening and understanding for a collective purpose.

CHAPTER FOUR
COMMUNICATIONS

I thought I understood what you said, but I just understood what I wanted to hear.
- Winston Churchill

When people say, It's not what you know, but who you know, they tell you that your network is more valuable than all those hours you spent binge-watching educational YouTube videos. It's about your interpersonal skills and getting along! And that's where effective communication comes in, saving the day like a hero in a dazzling cape and tights.

Workplace communication refers to communication at work about work. Knowing when and how to communicate at work effectively helps reduce delays caused by miscommunication, bolster collaboration, and foster trust. This includes discussing tasks, sharing projects, or giving feedback to managers or employees. Knowing how to communicate in the workplace is a vital part of effective collaboration—because if you can't communicate clearly, you risk miscommunication, confusion, or even unintentionally hurting someone's feelings. But building good communication habits takes time and effort—and that's where we come in.

Strong working relationships and productive productivity depend on effective communication at every level of an organization. This relevance has grown because of the Covid-19 outbreak, which forced many professionals to switch to remote work quickly.

Investing in effective communication cannot be emphasized in this new remote work scenario. Employers who take the time and try to create open lines of communication can quickly build trust among their workers. This trust motivates improved morale, increased output, and heightened productivity. Employees that can effectively communicate with coworkers, bosses, and clients are in high demand by any firm. When seeking employment prospects in a competitive market, this talent frequently becomes a differentiating feature for individuals.

Poor workplace communication can result in unmotivated employees who eventually mistrust their abilities and the firm. Fostering effective communication should be a key component of your organizational strategy for these five crucial reasons:

Building a team: Effective teams are built on collaboration and communication. To build strong teams, it is essential to use the tactics for improving communication described below. Improved morale and greater employee satisfaction follow from this.

Employee empowerment: Regarding their ideas or complaints, feeling heard and acknowledged is crucial to employee satisfaction. Open communication lines should enable everyone to interact freely with subordinates, superiors, and peers regardless of their place in the hierarchy.

Innovation: Ideas can flourish in a culture that promotes open communication without concern for punishment. This climate fosters innovation, and businesses that value communication are more likely to lead technological advancements.

Growth: Communication occurs both inside and outside of a company. The exterior message is kept consistent through internal coherence and strong communication channels. Growth projects place a significant emphasis on effective communication to ensure alignment among all stakeholders, internal and external.

Effective Management: Team leaders benefit from managers who are excellent communicators. Strong communication abilities significantly enhance task delegation, conflict resolution, motivation, and connection building—all essential for good management. Effective communication involves more than speaking; it also involves enabling people to interact with one another and establishing reliable communication channels.

Consider these actions to improve your organization's communication strategies:

Establish Realistic Goals: Managers must communicate realistic goals to teams and individuals while articulating project needs. The goals of the project, the department, and the organization should all be known to everyone.

Clarity: Create communications understandable to the target audience. This ensures your message is received clearly and without offending or confusing anyone.

Pick Your Medium Wisely: Decide which format best conveys your message. Face-to-face conversation promotes trust. However, alternative formats like printed materials or emails may also be helpful, depending on the situation.

Keep Communication Channels Accessible: Maintain open lines of communication. Encourage regular progress reports, which is essential when working with remote employees.

Communication is a discourse, so pay attention and be empathic. Respect is demonstrated by employers and businesses who solicit feedback and actively listen to it. This procedure aids in finding and resolving persisting problems.

When giving feedback to coworkers or employees, consider using the DiSC model in addition to the techniques. The DISC model was previously mentioned; details can be found on websites and reference books.

This strategy improves communication efficiency and fosters a pleasant and successful work atmosphere.

Here are tips on workplace communication that will outlast any virus.

Tip # 1: Be impeccable with your words, as suggested by Don Juan Ruiz. Words have power and can be used to disempower. Your word develops trust or distrust, so it is best to be honest when communicating with others to build trust. Various scientific studies show positive words are healthy, so sprinkle positivity like confetti.

Tip #2: Be clear and concise. No one wants to decode your message like they're solving a cryptic crossword puzzle. Skip the jargon and fancy lingo and get straight to the point. Remember, brevity is the soul of wit. Please keep it simple. You do not want to overload your employees and confuse them on their priorities or delay results like a game of charades.

Tip #3: Be specific. Don't be that person who says, I need help and leaves everyone scratching their heads like confused monkeys. Be more like a GPS that gives turn-by-turn directions. Say something like, Hey, I'm stuck on this report. Can you help me figure out how to calculate the total sales for the quarter? Being specific and sticking to facts can get you the right help. Avoid adding your interpretation or opinion to the facts.

Tip #4: Be positive. Even when delivering bad news, channel your inner Mary Poppins and add a spoonful of sugar or Tequila. Nobody wants to feel like they've been hit by a ton of bricks. So, wrap that negative message in a warm, fluffy blanket of positivity. Trust this; your colleagues will thank you for sparing their delicate emotions.

Tip #5: Be respectful. Like that golden rule, your grandma taught you: Treat others how you want to be treated. Don't unleash your inner Hulk when you disagree with someone. Keep those insults and name-calling in your imaginary wrestling ring. Instead, practice the art of polite disagreement and show that you're a mature, responsible adult (even if you still laugh at fart jokes).

Tip #6: Be open to feedback. Newsflash: you could be better. Shocking, I know! Nobody is. So, when someone offers you feedback, resist the urge to turn into a defensive armadillo. Instead, open your mind and ears and be willing to learn and grow. It builds collaboration skills and compromise. Be a good listener and be respectful of others' ideas. Thank the person for their feedback, and let them know you appreciate their help. Embrace feedback like a gift from the communication gods.

Tip #7: Know where and when to communicate. If the message is uplifting for a team member, it can be in an open area. If the message is neutral or concerns one person, the conversation may be best in private to save face. Understand the different communication channels your company uses and when to use each. Talk face-to-face when you can, as it is often the best way to communicate your message. It's also an excellent way to build relationships with your colleagues.

Tip #8: Align your body language with what you're saying, and be open and welcoming. Remember, actions speak louder than words, so ensure your body isn't sending mixed signals. No more saying, I'm totally on board while crossing your arms and rolling your eyes. Instead, show some enthusiasm, stand tall, nod in agreement, and watch your colleagues do a double take as they wonder about the assertiveness you've mastered. Watch your body language and tone of voice, which can communicate as much as your words.

Tip #9: Respect gender differences in communication strategies and adapt. Yes, ladies and gentlemen, our communication code sometimes needs cracking. When a female coworker presents an issue, don't jump straight into solution mode like a tech support hotline. Take a page from the book of open-ended questions and let her explore her thoughts. And folks, remember that a head nod might be seen as agreement by one but as attentive listening by another. Yes, it will take time since men are from Venus and women are from Mars. Oh, and some are from Uranus, where I hope we will get this gender communication dance down to a science someday!

Tip #10: Develop an appreciation for cultural differences and interact productively with diverse individuals. The workplace is a melting pot of cultures, so embrace diversity like a delicious international potluck. Language barriers, gestures, and customs may throw you off balance, but fear not! Embrace the opportunity to learn from each other. Be mindful of the audience you're communicating with and tailor your message. Remember, the world would be boring if we communicated the same way. So, embrace the cultural flavors and sprinkle international spice into your conversations.

Tip #11: Reduce reliance on technology and prioritize interpersonal interaction. We live in the age of screens, where emojis have replaced actual emotions. We've become keyboard robots, firing emails and instant messages faster than a caffeinated cheetah. But let's remember the joy of face-to-face interactions. Step away from the screens and engage in some good old-fashioned human connection. Not only will it make your workplace livelier, but it'll also give your eyes a break from those dreaded blue light rays.

Tip #12: Accept constructive criticism and offer it when appropriate. That's right, feedback. It can be as delicate as balancing a tower of Jenga blocks while riding a unicycle. Instead of getting defensive like a porcupine on a rollercoaster, embrace constructive criticism. And when it's your turn to offer constructive criticism, remember to sprinkle it with kindness and wrap it in a sandwich of kindness. Nobody likes explosive feedback!

Tip #13: Maintain neutrality in your communication, like the country of Switzerland. Stay calm, relaxed, and collected like a cucumber on ice if you're in a heated discussion at work with emotions running high. Avoid taking sides in office dramas or heated debates. Instead, play the role of the neutral observer, sipping your neutral-grounded tea and watching the drama unfold. You'll become the office Zen master quickly.

Tip #14: Be a good listener by repeating what employees say to understand their statements. This means only interrupting them if you seek clarification. Interrupting can create a soap opera. Let them finish their thought and be in the spotlight before you swoop in to get enlightened or turn out the lights.

Tip #15: do not make assumptions, as Don Juan Ruiz states in the four agreements. Assumptions may be far from the truth. Ruiz discusses how often we assume that may lead to suffering and immediately believe it is true. We must justify everything, explain and understand everything, and feel safe. We have millions of questions that need answers because there are so many things that the reasoning mind can't explain. It is not essential if the answer is correct; the answer itself makes us feel safe. You know what they say about assumptions—it makes an ass out of you and me. So, ditch the crystal ball and mind-reading attempts. Ask questions, clarify, and be Sherlock Holmes when understanding what others think or feel.

Tip #16: Be bigger, and do not take things personally. We often feel hurt, angry, and frustrated when we take things personally. This can lead to increased stress and anxiety. By learning not to take things personally, we can reduce these negative emotions and improve our overall mental health. If someone says something that rubs you the wrong way, take a deep breath and resist the urge to unleash your inner Hulk. Instead, channel your inner Dalai Lama and seek understanding: compassion and patience, my friend.

Tip #17: Remember that everyone is different. What one person says or does may not be hurtful, but it can still be interpreted that way. Remember that everyone has a unique perspective and communication. Be aware of your triggers and those of others.

Tip #18: Collaboration is working together to achieve a common goal. It can involve people from different departments, teams, or even organizations. The benefits are increased productivity, improved decision-making, innovation, learning, and morale.

Tip #19: Be persistent and do not give up. Communication can be as tricky as solving a Rubik's Cube blindfolded. Life is all about persistence! So, keep trying different approaches, like a scientist experimenting in a lab, until you find the magic formula that clicks with the person you're communicating with. Keep going even if you don't see results immediately. Just keep working at it, and you'll eventually see improvement. Effective communication takes time and practice.

Tip #20: Success is not a solo vessel. If you need help with your communication skills, get help. There are many resources available to help you improve your communication skills. Talk to your manager, a mentor, or a communication coach.

Tip #21: Some employees have anger issues, and if yelling starts, stay calm and respectful. Listen to what the employee is saying; even if you disagree, listening to what they must say is essential. Acknowledge the person's feelings. Offer a solution or an apology if appropriate. But document the incident, whether with a boss or colleague. When confronted with yelling or extreme tension, our brains enter flight, fight, or freeze mode. It's like a mini-Jurassic Park in our heads, with cortisol, the stress hormone, playing the role of the T-Rex. So, when your boss is roaring like a T-Rex, remember to keep your cool and protect that precious logical thinking.

Effective communication is like the secret sauce of workplace success. Add the magical ingredient to turn your interactions from a bologna sandwich into a delicatessen feast. So, go forth armed with these tips, and conquer communication with charisma because it's how we build trust, collaborate, and solve problems among our colleagues, clients, and customers.

CHAPTER
FIVE
BALANCING DIVERSITY

The universe is a symphony of differences, and each of us is a unique note. - Thich Nhat Hanh

Diversity is a vast puzzle of parallels and variances, with a sprinkle of uniqueness in every corner of the workforce. We've got folks from various social, cultural, and personal backgrounds, each bringing their spice to the mix. We've got age, gender, sexual orientation, attitudes, abilities, religious views, races, ages, ethnicities, athletic prowess! —you name it! It's like a vibrant mosaic filled with intriguing qualities, making our modern workplace much more enjoyable.

Let's value both our differences and similarities like the true diversity enthusiasts we are! When our workplace is inclusive, everyone feels appreciated, respected, and accepted for who they are. It's like a warm hug from the whole team! And guess what? When people feel valued and recognized, they become superstars at work! They're driven, they're motivated, and they contribute to the business like nobody's business! But let's not forget that when we exclude or act prejudiced, we're like a dark cloud raining on someone's parade. They feel frustrated, stressed, and even angrier than a tea kettle without a lid.

So, how do we create this beautiful harmony in our workplace? Well, that's where diversity management comes in! It's like a carefully crafted recipe of assorted chocolates—many origins, experiences, and viewpoints to ensure everyone's talents bring good taste. The real trick is to tap into everyone's talents and make the most of this diverse bunch. We want a positive work atmosphere where all those viewpoints are acknowledged and celebrated! Each person's unique abilities are like puzzle pieces that fit perfectly into the company's big picture.

Managers and leaders must navigate through the many facets of diversity with grace and understanding. They've got to encourage an inclusive culture where diversity is cherished and every worker feels like a valued part of the team. Thanks to cultural shifts, globalization, and incredible technological breakthroughs, demographics are evolving faster than a downhill roller coaster. Leadership requires acknowledging legislative changes that support equality and inclusivity. Their support for diversity initiatives sets the tone for an inclusive and welcoming workplace.

Many of the USA's Fortune 500 CEO or CFO are more diverse through opportunity. Who knew having a diverse workforce would be like having a secret weapon of innovation, creativity, and problem-solving? We unlock a new level of success by encouraging open communication and listening to all those varied cultural voices.

Success is having a diverse team that can turbocharge a company's market reach and customer satisfaction. When our team understands different cultural backgrounds, we can serve clients and consumers like never. With the proper senior management and diversity management techniques, there are no limits in this fast-paced world.

Every company should want to create a place where everyone feels like they belong, no matter where they come from, to make it the heart of their culture in building bridges. That means changing old structures and procedures to fit our new goals. We're reevaluating hiring practices, promoting fairness, and saying goodbye to discrimination.

You don't need a pilot's license to fly into training for cultural sensitivity and diversity awareness! It's a way to understand and appreciate different points of view. Breaking down stereotypes with open conversations makes our workplace peaceful and inclusive. A most welcoming and effective workplace happens when we embrace diversity. Everyone feels like they belong and can contribute their best when we're not just focusing on individual differences but taking in the beautiful life source, bringing fresh ideas, creativity, and problem-solving skills.

By embracing diversity in the hiring process, we're opening doors to a talent pool of amazing people. Take pleasure in the hunt for unique skill sets and experiences. We're not limiting ourselves but casting the net broad and catching uniqueness. With a diverse team, we can connect with different target markets like never. It's like having a universal translator that speaks all languages and understands all cultures. We will make our customers feel understood and appreciated.

A diverse workforce allows employees to meet people from all corners of the world with different cultures, customs, and practices. It's like going on a global vacation without leaving the office! This exposure to different ideas broadens our understanding of the world and makes us more open-minded adventurers. Looking at actions and behaviors differently is like discovering a new world of other people's motivations and struggles.

We have the recipe for team success: clear purpose and value are the main ingredients. Add a dash of empowerment and a generous serving of open communication. Stir in robust connections and flexibility, and watch the success flourish. Sprinkle some maximum productivity and top it off with appreciation and acknowledgment. There's more—we've got open communication, robust connections, flexibility, and maximum productivity.

Leadership starts with creating a culture of appreciation and acceptance for good morale. It's like exploring the many cultural backgrounds present in our organization and celebrating the uniqueness of each individual. We're trying to banish prejudices and embrace diversity like a warm hug.

A diversity program starts with finding similarities and differences in our workforce. Explore a treasure trove of unique attributes and determine how they affect our current procedures. Second, we give change enough time to marinate and settle in discussing and establishing essential adjustments with enough time to spare. And last but not least, it is an ongoing process intertwined with continuous management and communication. When there are anti-diversity problems, take a four-step solution: containment, reframing, processing, and release.

Dealing with affirmative action can be an adventure taking specific corrective efforts to redress demographic imbalances. Communication is key. Many agencies need to work on assuming management is right before identifying the issues and fairness, which may take a minor issue into a more extensive and costlier realm. Not all management decisions are righteous. It is best to recognize issues, secure leadership commitment, create tailored solutions, establish essential goals, and watch the progress while adjusting our corporate culture and leading the way with active leadership. Diversity is a strategic advantage, like a secret weapon that boosts productivity, innovation, and overall performance.

Managing diversity in the workplace is no walk in the park, be ready to ride the ups and downs. Anticipate potential obstacles in our planning stage. By doing so, we reduce stress and activate our proactive problem-solving methods.

Managing diversity in the workplace is no walk in the park, but we're ready to ride the ups and downs. Diversity is here to stay as we adjust Post-COVID to remote work and flexible office formats. Our hybrid workplace prioritizes making everyone feel appreciated and engaged with a sense of belonging. Increased retention, productivity, and morale can be achieved with diversity. With remote work and virtual communication, we have a passport to virtual assistants embracing various cultures and adapting to different markets.

In the grand finale, we celebrate the Unity of Diversity! Organizational climate embraces and promotes diversity, challenging prejudices along the way. Leaders take the spotlight, recognizing the varied cultures within the workforce and creating a welcoming workplace. By embracing diversity, you can create a masterpiece—a staff that thrives in the contemporary workplace's varied environment.

CHAPTER SIX
EMPLOYING CHANGE WITH ZEN

Work is love made visible. - Kahlil Gibran

In the ever-changing landscape of the post-COVID workplace, maintaining a Zen mindset is essential for navigating the shifting dynamics with grace and resilience. This chapter explores how the principles of Zen can help individuals embrace change, build strong professional relationships, and foster a peaceful work environment. Through the following subchapters, we will delve into various aspects of Zen and provide real-life examples to illustrate their practical application.

Openness and Sincerity

Zen principles prioritize openness and sincerity in professional relationships. By being forthright and honest in all interactions, we create an environment where people feel safe to share their thoughts and ideas. For instance, instead of engaging in harmful behaviors like gossiping or dishonesty, let's encourage open communication and keep our promises. Embodying these qualities inspires those around us to do the same. Remember the advice of Don Miguel Ruiz, Keep your words impeccable (unless someone asks you if you approve of their attire).

A manager could set an example of openness and sincerity by sharing their thoughts and feelings with their team. This could create a culture of trust and transparency where everyone feels comfortable sharing their ideas and opinions.

Healthy Boundaries

Setting clear boundaries is crucial when dealing with difficult coworkers. It allows us to address disrespectful conduct while maintaining our self-worth and pride. Communicating firmly but respectfully establishes that abusive behavior will not be tolerated. Real-life examples could include scenarios where individuals stand up for themselves while maintaining professionalism, such as firmly but respectfully addressing a colleague's derogatory comments. A touch of humor can lighten the mood while getting the point across if you must leave a note for the refrigerator monster or not reimbursing the coffee can.

A coworker could set a clear boundary by refusing to engage in gossip or drama. This would show they are unwilling to tolerate disrespectful behavior, and it would set an excellent example for others.

Mutual Aid and Assistance

Zen Buddhism emphasizes the value of collaboration and mutual support. Prioritizing group efforts over individual accomplishments fosters an environment of trust and appreciation. By looking for ways to lend a hand to our coworkers, we contribute to a culture of teamwork. Real-life examples could highlight where individuals help their colleagues, improving cooperation and overall team performance.

A team could collaborate on a project by sharing their skills and resources. This would help them to achieve their goals more quickly and efficiently.

Stability and Equanimity

Mastering stability and equanimity in the workplace are core tenets of Zen. By practicing self-control and avoiding personal biases and emotional responses, we can make sound judgments and promote effective communication. Real-life examples could illustrate situations where individuals remain calm and objective in facing challenges, allowing for fair resolutions and maintaining a peaceful work environment.

A leader could demonstrate stability and equanimity by remaining calm and collected in the face of challenges. This would help to keep the team focused and productive.

Appreciation and Gratitude

Expressing appreciation and gratitude towards our employer and colleagues creates a positive and inspiring work environment. Acknowledging their efforts and contributions publicly fosters a sense of community and boosts team spirit. Real-life examples could showcase instances where individuals publicly recognize their coworkers' achievements, leading to increased motivation and a stronger sense of belonging.

A company could show appreciation for its employees by giving them regular feedback and rewards. This would help to motivate employees and boost morale.

Mindful Communication

Mindfulness plays a vital role in maintaining a Zen attitude in the workplace. Mindful listening skills help us understand others' perspectives and foster mutual understanding. We create a space for open and civil conversation by listening without interrupting or passing judgment. Real-life examples could highlight instances where individuals practice mindful communication during challenging discussions, leading to improved understanding and problem-solving.

A customer service representative could practice mindful communication by listening carefully to customers' concerns. This would help to resolve issues more quickly and efficiently.

Adaptability and Growth Mindset

Embracing change and having a growth mindset is essential in the modern workplace. A Zen mindset views change as an opportunity for personal development and growth, allowing individuals to adapt to new situations with enthusiasm and tenacity. Real-life examples could feature individuals who embrace change, willingly learn new skills, and adapt to evolving work environments, demonstrating the benefits of a growth mindset.

A new employee could demonstrate adaptability and a growth mindset by being willing to learn new skills and take on new challenges. This would show they are committed to their career and willing to grow.

Self-Awareness and Mindfulness Practices

Self-awareness and mindfulness are crucial for maintaining stability and serenity in uncertain times. Individuals can effectively cope with stress and remain grounded by cultivating a sense of inner calm and clarity. Mindfulness practices such as meditation, deep breathing, and regular breaks help individuals stay focused and resilient. Real-life examples could showcase individuals incorporating mindfulness practices into their daily work routines, leading to improved well-being and performance.

A manager could incorporate mindfulness practices into their daily routine by taking breaks and practicing deep breathing. This would help them to stay focused and reduce stress.

Building Solid Connections

Establishing solid connections with coworkers fosters a supportive work environment. By listening, appreciating unique perspectives, and showing empathy, individuals can create a sense of community and belonging. Real-life examples highlight instances where individuals foster strong connections through open dialogue and collaboration, leading to increased cooperation and productivity.

A team could build solid connections by organizing social events and opportunities for employees to get to know each other better. This would help to create a sense of community and belonging.

Recognizing and Rewarding Success

Recognizing and rewarding individual and team achievements promotes a positive and motivating work environment. By acknowledging the efforts of others, individuals feel appreciated and inspired. Real-life examples could feature organizations that regularly celebrate successes, fostering a culture of appreciation and boosting morale.

A company could recognize and reward success by celebrating team wins and individual achievements. This would help to motivate employees and boost morale.

Constructive Feedback and Continuous Improvement

Providing constructive feedback and opportunities for improvement is integral to maintaining a Zen mindset. Individuals can learn and grow by receiving and responding to constructive criticism in a supportive and encouraging manner. Real-life examples could demonstrate instances where individuals embrace feedback, leading to personal growth and enhanced performance.

A manager could provide constructive feedback by focusing on the positive and offering suggestions for improvement. This would help employees to learn and grow.

∞

By integrating Zen principles into the workplace, individuals can navigate the post-COVID dynamics with resilience and well-being. Combining openness, sincerity, healthy boundaries, mutual aid, stability, appreciation, mindful communication, adaptability, self-awareness, solid connections, recognition, and continuous improvement cultivates a Zen mindset that promotes personal and professional growth. Embracing Zen is not a fad but an essential strategy for flourishing in a changing work landscape while finding purpose and fulfillment.

The best way to find yourself is to lose yourself in the service of others. - Mahatma Gandhi.

CHAPTER SEVEN
UTILIZING ARTIFICIAL INTELLIGENCE

The greatest intelligence is to know when you have enough. - Lao Tzu

Unprecedented difficulties brought on by the COVID-19 epidemic forced nations to stop its spread. While many businesses switched to remote employment, crucial industries like healthcare, transportation, and manufacturing supported society. Temperature scanning became essential for locating potentially contaminated people among the containment gear. However, this method has drawbacks like calibration problems and human error. This section examines how artificial intelligence (AI) has transformed pandemic response tactics, including everything from autonomous temperature assessment to accelerated drug research and improved last-mile delivery safety.

Businesses and communities hurried to implement temperature screening using contactless thermometers in the early phases of the pandemic. Despite these attempts, there was still viral propagation because of calibration errors and the possibility of human mistakes. This process underwent a paradigm shift with the introduction of AI, with sophisticated AI models replacing imperfect human supervision. Thousands of people's temperatures can be swiftly and correctly assessed by these models every hour, alerting authorities to suspected instances practically immediately. This proactive strategy supports efforts to reduce the risk of transmission and makes it possible for speedier reaction actions in high-traffic areas like malls, hospitals, and offices.

Additionally, AI-driven cameras offer comprehensive safety solutions beyond temperature detection. About following attendance rules, these cameras keep an eye on the number of people in the room, immediately notifying the appropriate parties about unruly crowd sizes. Additionally, AI models enforce safety rules like mask use and social distance, spotting non-compliance and enabling prompt correction. Employing AI technologies helps organizations and agencies allocate employees more efficiently and improve overall safety compliance.

AI affects efforts to find COVID-19 medicines that work. Moderna and other medical businesses use AI and machine learning to hasten the development of medications and vaccines. These technologies accelerate the identification and testing of viable candidates, potentially reducing mortality rates and the virus's long-term consequences. A further benefit of AI's predictive powers is the ability to foresee virus changes and their possible effects on transmission, severity, and the effectiveness of treatments. AI is a critical tool for understanding mutation trends and optimizing containment techniques as scientists worldwide battle emerging outbreaks.

Due to the increased need for socially isolated services, the pandemic increased last-mile deliveries. To accommodate this demand, inexperienced drivers entered the workforce, necessitating increased traffic safety measures. With the help of AI, advanced driver assistance systems (ADAS) and driver monitoring systems (DMS) have become crucial tools for reducing operating hazards. Using quick feedback to correct behavior and ensure scrupulous adherence to safety rules, these systems train and supervise new drivers.

Using AI is crucial in developing efficient pandemic responses as the epidemic changes our global landscape. AI's uses are numerous and crucial, from autonomous temperature assessment to expediting treatment research and enhancing traffic safety. As obstacles change, AI-driven solutions substantially contribute to public safety, research acceleration, and operational optimization, providing a guiding light for organizations, governments, and people navigating these uncharted waters.

CHAPTER
EIGHT
PREPARING FOR PHENOMENON

Treat every moment as your last. It is not preparation for something else. - Shunryu Suzuki

The wisdom encapsulated in Suzuki's quote above holds a profound lesson about the significance of living in the present. At first glance, this advice might seem counterintuitive, as it suggests focusing on the present moment rather than preparing for the future. However, upon deeper reflection, we can uncover a layer of insight that touches on both the present and the future.

When we approach every moment as if it were our last, we immerse ourselves fully in the present experience. We savor each interaction, sensation, and emotion, recognizing each moment's beauty and depth. This practice cultivates mindfulness and a profound connection with the current reality, allowing us to experience life's richness without distraction or preoccupation with future events.

Yet, Suzuki's words also remind us that living in the present is not an isolated endeavor. While we treat each moment as our last, we simultaneously lay the foundation for an uncertain future. Every moment we embrace, and every lesson we learn contributes to our personal growth and resilience. These moments of presence become building blocks, shaping our responses to future phenomena, challenges, or emergencies. In this way, the act of treating every moment as the last is not separate from preparing for the future; it is the most genuine and effective form of preparation.

Suzuki's guidance encourages us to recognize our present experiences' interconnectedness and readiness for the unknown. By embracing the present moment with mindfulness and gratitude, we equip ourselves with a deep reservoir of wisdom, strength, and adaptability we can draw upon when unforeseen circumstances arise. Ultimately, his message underscores the idea that living in the present is not just a way to cherish life—the practice fortifies us to face future uncertainties with courage and resilience.

The need to prepare our workplaces for pandemics and emergencies has grown in an ever-changing world where the need to be ready for unforeseen difficulties is crucial. The recent global events have highlighted how susceptible companies and organizations are to unexpected disruptions, emphasizing the importance of having solid backup plans and flexible strategies.

Preparing the workplace for pandemics and emergencies emerges as both a relevant worry and a fundamental responsibility as we traverse a terrain where uncertainty is the new norm. This chapter digs into the preventive measures, resilient practices, and creative solutions to build workplaces that can weather impending storms, protecting employees' safety and the continuity of business operations.

Business executives are heaving a sigh of relief as the covid variant outbreak slips into history thanks to improved community immunity, new efficient treatments, and the accessibility of numerous diagnostics and vaccines. However, the pandemic is far from over, given the appearance of the Omicron BA.2 strain and its following mutations and the gradually eroding protection from infections and immunizations.

Companies must be ready to meet any problems the pandemic may provide in this dynamic and unexpected environment. This chapter offers brief instructions describing four crucial steps that executives may take right away to improve worker safety and reduce business interruptions in the event of future community breakouts.

The global situation is still unclear as Covid-19 instances sharply increased in March across Europe and have since persisted in several regions of Asia and North America, along with worrying forecasts of an approaching fall surge from U.S. officials. The remaining country with a zero-tolerance stance against the coronavirus, China, struggles with containment measures.

Beyond the current situation, it is crucial to recognize the potential for additional Covid-19 breakouts or waves. The SARS-CoV-2 virus causes Covid-19 and can spread between humans and mammals, resulting in frequently unpredictable changes. Given their limited access to diagnostic procedures, immunizations, and sufficient quarantine measures, the flood of over 5.2 million Ukrainian conflict refugees poses a heightened global risk. Concurrently, the risk of transmission might be increased by the deterioration of immunity to the virus or any of its variations resistant to standard vaccines.

Epidemic weariness has affected not only the general people but even business executives after fighting the epidemic and its changing strains for more than two years. These company leaders want to focus their knowledge and resources on critical business areas while putting less thought, time, and effort into pandemic worries. However, the answer isn't to ignore the pandemic but to build a solid mechanism to control it. These system's essential elements should include:

Employers have selectively relaxed pandemic-related safeguards given the present low rates of community transmission throughout most of the United States, encouraging a balance between safety and the freedom for workers to socialize and produce at their best. Many businesses are allowing remote workers back into the office due to decreased infection risk, and most have eliminated mask requirements.

Employers must continue with basic safety procedures even when restrictions are reduced. These procedures include promoting the proper immunizations or boosters, advising sick workers to stay at home, enhancing indoor air quality, and keeping a system alerting employees to potential exposure. Further, protective measures can be modified following new municipal, state, or federal regulations as necessary.

Even if local public health recommendations require it, keeping indoor masking a choice for everyone is crucial. Managers should avoid assuming things about people who wear masks. Creating an atmosphere that encourages employee self-defense improves well-being in the short term and prevents potential interruptions brought on by illnesses.

Given how quickly a novel coronavirus variation might spread throughout the globe, businesses want dependable protocols to protect their operations from impending outbreaks. Employers have a rare opportunity to put the priceless knowledge gained over the last two years into developing plans aligned with the pandemic landscape by taking advantage of the current phase, distinguished by low transmission rates.

A successful response must contain several essential components. Finding the indicators and thresholds that cause changes to the company's Covid-19 safety procedures is a wise place to start. Businesses can build triggers that specify the correct responses by considering variables like community transmission rates, hospital capacity, wastewater surveillance, variation infectivity, test positivity rates, and vaccination coverage.

Additionally, businesses need to decide which locations require monitoring. While many firms should limit monitoring activities to locations with sizable employee populations and data that can be easily accessed, in other circumstances, assessing the risk of employee homes may be more important than reviewing the actual work site. The key is identifying locations where a sizable portion of the workforce is present or where minimizing business disruption is still essential.

Most interventions, including mask use, education about the effectiveness of various mask types, physical separation, Covid-19 testing, and vaccine requirements, can be adjusted to change in response to changing conditions. However, too many changes too frequently can cause employees to get confused about the current rules. Organizations can respond quickly to developments with less need for new decision-making when they take a well-established, balanced strategy. Businesses that embrace streamlined plans have an advantage over rivals forced to create reactive answers for every epidemic turn.

Numerous businesses continue to provide the option of remote work because they understand the advantages it provides to both the company and its employees. This flexibility is especially crucial for unvaccinated or high-risk individuals, such as those with weakened immune systems. To do this, employers should create improved policies for on-site non-immune or unvaccinated workers, such as promoting ongoing remote work, requiring indoor masking, or implementing surveillance testing.

Companies have cleverly encouraged collaboration and community in remote or hybrid work environments. Some businesses encourage in-office attendance on particular workdays of the week or plan special events and staff get-togethers to enhance camaraderie while reducing transmission risks. Given that modern workers actively seek adaptive organizations delivering stability during turbulent times, businesses that continue to support adaptable work arrangements will undoubtedly be better positioned to draw in and keep talent.

Even when community incidence rates are still low, the lingering possibility of localized outbreaks or surges highlights the importance of continued communication with employees. In line with a survey done this winter, employees believe their companies did an excellent job of protecting their well-being throughout the epidemic. Additionally, workers who felt their employers prioritized workplace safety showed higher levels of engagement, increased productivity, and a lower risk of leaving. Additionally, some workers might doubt the necessity of reintroducing pandemic safety precautions, which emphasizes the value of open communication and the part managers and other leaders play in defining employee expectations.

Even if they admit that fewer precautions are necessary when there are low community case rates, employers can still provide regular updates on the company's safety approach. These contacts ought to be regular and timed to the local conditions. If conditions change, this established framework for communication lays the path for prompt company-wide reactions.

Although it can take years to establish credibility and trust among coworkers, these ties can break down in days or weeks. A crucial component in maintaining employee trust and resilience in the face of future challenges is communicating a painstakingly prepared pandemic safety strategy openly and honestly.

A rare opportunity exists for businesses to develop protocols and systems that manage potential pandemic threats at this crossroads, characterized by low risks but still ringing with memories of the Omicron wave. This preparation allows employers to focus on managing challenging economic and geopolitical situations. Through proactive, adaptable planning, businesses obtain a competitive edge that positions them competitively, regardless of the uncertainties that lie ahead.

Remember, the success of each country relies on various elements of its economy; the vision of entrepreneurs, the ideas of creative innovators, a healthy workforce, and the security and welfare of the labor market.

AFTERWORD

The best way to find yourself is to lose yourself in the service of others. - Mahatma Gandhi

We have traversed the terrain of workplace transformations, discovered the hidden treasures of personalities that lurk among us, and harnessed the mystical power of effective communication and understanding within our diverse teams. We even tapped into the ancient wisdom of Zen, wellness, and mindfulness to create a haven of tranquility amidst the chaotic office jungle.

Do not descend into the realm of seriousness! For what fun is life without a hearty dose of laughter and silliness? Let us revel in the eccentricities that make us delightfully unique as we gracefully conclude this extraordinary escapade. Remember, we have learned that forcing everyone into the same mold is as effective as trying to fit a square peg into a round hole during a cosmic alignment. Instead, let us celebrate the kaleidoscope of human characters, from the striking to the subtly peculiar, from the comedians who tickle our funny bones to the enigmatic souls who surprise us at every turn, confiscating our food from the snack room. Raise your cups high and toast to this marvelous symphony of oddity!

The key to everlasting joy in the workplace lies within the perfect blend of self-improvement, teamwork, and a generous sprinkling of optimism. It is akin to baking a cake from scratch! A positive outlook empowers us to triumph over any challenge that comes our way. With the knowledge and tools we have acquired on this enlightening journey, we can confidently navigate the winding paths of personal and professional growth.

But let us take a moment to breathe, for we have weathered the storm of uncertainty during the post-COVID era. Amidst the chaos of ringing phones and overflowing inboxes, we have discovered the strength to persevere and the serenity to find peace in constant interruptions. Wellness and Zen mindfulness have proven to be more than mere buzzwords; they are sensible elixirs of rejuvenation and stress relief. So, take a deep breath (now is a good time), close your eyes, and allow the waves of Zen to wash over you.

Now, you may wonder, what is the cherry atop this delectable sundae of wisdom? Together, we have unlocked the secrets to nurturing our Zen mindset for the long and whimsical journey ahead. By embracing self-care rituals, fostering supportive relationships, and reveling in the dance of delightful chaos, we have laid the foundation for a lifetime of happiness and fulfillment. So, my fellow adventurers in the office realm, let us venture forth armed with our newfound wisdom and sprinkle your Zen-like personality far and wide.

As we bid farewell to this voyage, let us remember to keep laughter in our hearts, growth in our souls, and appreciation for the marvelous individuals who grace our lives. We can weave a work environment that harmonizes productivity, joy, camaraderie, and triumph. Go forth on your journey with your Office Zen, and may it be filled with laughter, lightness, and a touch of delightful chaos. Here's to a future of fighting, flying, and, above all, fostering fellowship.

The journey of a thousand miles begins with a single step. - Lao Tzu

THANK YOU

Please leave a One-Click Review.

Customer reviews
★★★★★ 5 out of 5
14 customer ratings

5 star		100%
4 star		0%
3 star		0%
2 star		0%
1 star		0%

Review this product
Share your thoughts with other customers

[Write a customer review]

And possibly a few words

I sincerely thank you for your journey with me through the pages of this book. Your time is precious. It would be an immense gift if you could spare a moment to leave a review on www.Amazon.com. Reviews breathe life into the work of authors like myself. Readers like you make the challenging journey of writing so rewarding.

If you have questions or wish to delve deeper into the subject discussed, I am more than eager to engage in that dialogue. Don't hesitate to get in touch with me at sam.c.martinez@gmail.com. Although my travels might sometimes delay me, your message will receive my attention at the earliest opportunity.

As we venture into life's journey, let us embrace our boundless potential, unhindered by the chains of prejudice or the limitations of any individual or institution. May we rise, empowered by our inner strength and fueled by our dreams, living each day to the fullest and reminding the world of the incredible beings we will be. Life is a blessing.

SAMUEL C MARTINEZ

> To find the secrets of the Universe, think in terms
> of frequency, energy, and vibration.
>
> — *Nicola Tesla*

Made in the USA
Columbia, SC
19 September 2023